I0884876

ABANDONED ALABAMA

DARK SHADOWS OF GENERATIONS PAST

JAY FARRELL

AMERICA THROUGH TIME®
ADDING COLOR TO AMERICAN HISTORY

America Through Time is an imprint of Fonthill Media LLC
www.through-time.com
office@through-time.com

Published by Arcadia Publishing by arrangement with Fonthill Media LLC
For all general information, please contact Arcadia Publishing:
Telephone: 843-853-2070
Fax: 843-853-0044
E-mail: sales@arcadiapublishing.com
For customer service and orders:
Toll-Free 1-888-313-2665

www.arcadiapublishing.com

First published 2019

Copyright © Jay Farrell 2019

ISBN 978-1-63499-161-2

All rights reserved. No part of this publication may be reproduced, stored in a retrieval system or transmitted in any form or by any means, electronic, mechanical, photocopying, recording or otherwise, without prior permission in writing from Fonthill Media LLC

Typeset in Trade Gothic 10pt on 15pt
Printed and bound in England

CONTENTS

About the Author **4**

Introduction **5**

1 Beginner's Luck **7**

2 Hot Property **13**

3 Farmhouse Folklore **17**

4 The Asylum **26**

5 American as Apple Pie **52**

6 Pour Yourself a Drink **56**

7 Life on the Farm **62**

8 Yesterday's Newspaper **69**

9 The Victorian Inn **72**

10 The Road to Vernon **81**

11 Nestled in the Pines **87**

More by Jay Farrell **95**

ABOUT THE AUTHOR

Jay Farrell is a Nashville, Tennessee, based photographer who loves photographing abandoned structures. He has a passion for utilizing his camera to share the unique, distressed beauty of abandoned homes and structures that most of the world has forgotten. Sharing his adventures with the public through authorship and blogging inspires him as much as the adventures themselves.

INTRODUCTION

The "life after people" feel to abandoned buildings—complete with rotted and caving floors, forgotten contents of yesteryear, and the overall entropy and distress—are what fuels my inspiration. There's a freedom (and a danger) of hitting the open road and exploring the backroad to seek these abandoned treasures. These structures tell a story. My goal while photographing these structures is to tell those stories and be their voice after they've been forgotten, sometimes for generations.

There is a process to my work. I don't force my way in or vandalize and I don't take or disturb anything. This shows a level of respect and reduces liability. These places are sometimes a hideout for squatters or vandals, which adds potential danger to the situation. It's extremely rare to be confronted by an heir or property owner, but it can happen. The structures are dangerous, with roofs caving in, broken glass, nails, needles, wildlife, loose boards, and weak floors. You must know what is under your feet—another reason I prefer to go with a trusted colleague if that option is available. It's eerie; there are lots of noises, creaks, and constant echoes.

This book features the work from my travels and adventures in Alabama. I will take you with me on the journey through some of the most dilapidated structures that most people only imagine. You will enjoy an exciting mix of old bygone farmhouses nestled in the woods and cotton fields, and the chilling adventure documenting an abandoned insane asylum.

It's not for the faint of heart, but the walls always tell stories and I enjoy the adventures. In this book, I will make my audience part of the adventure. I take you up close and personal to these tumbling structures, far deeper than the roadside view. Through my lens, you will experience the true feel of Sweet Home Alabama. I hope you enjoy it!

1

BEGINNER'S LUCK

There are days when we wake up and randomly decide that some impromptu, random exploration is what our creative, free-spirited souls need. This was one of those days. It was a rainy autumn day in Nashville, which would have made local exploration a bust. My last excursion in Alabama left me with a taste for more. The weather was overcast in Northern Alabama, but not raining. I packed a sandwich, my adventurous spirit, plenty of water, and seized my opportunity. I was curious about the Northern Alabama towns near Tennessee, since I had a free afternoon, but not the entire day.

After exiting the interstate, the first thing I did was pick a direction, looking for backroads to explore off the beaten path. Shortly into my journey, I saw an abandoned farmhouse that backed up to an active cotton field. The case is often that a previous generation lived in the house, while the land is still used by the family. The house becomes too much work to fix up, and it's either abandoned or used for farm storage. After all, it eats no hay.

Although I felt the tranquility of the quiet countryside, whistling wind, and the vast cotton fields, I knew there could have been eyes on me. It was time to continue my exploration elsewhere and not exhaust my resources further than I needed to. This charming old dilapidated farmhouse told a story of hard work, making an honest living, and a family coming together with home cooked meals every day. Perhaps someone living in the vicinity could tell us all about that house and the family who lived there. Sometimes I have access to those stories—other times the photos tell the only necessary story.

Above: An interesting perspective of the street view of the old farmhouse.

Left: Since there was a house across the road, I wanted to go around back so I'm not as easily seen. The side may be in an even worse state of disrepair than the front.

I've learned that there are no abandoned barns, unless they are in this poor of a condition.

The back side of the house, with nothing but the wind and open cotton field around me.

This barn that backed up to the cotton field makes a very picturesque landscape and architectural photograph. This is a vision that Americans in other regions of the country can only picture when they hear country music or watch old Western movies.

The view that caught my eye from the road. By that point, I knew there was not a way inside the house.

Part of a farm plow surrounded by overgrowth and this deteriorating house.

That's as far inside as I could get. There was no floor left, obstacles packed the house everywhere, and the windows were boarded up. It was as dark as a cave.

The door to the dark abyss.

2

HOT PROPERTY

As I continued my journey through Limestone County and Madison, my findings were a bit scarce. It was a large area that I just wanted to explore, and this game requires patience. I've mentioned this before—despite the stereotype about Alabama, you can't throw a dart in any direction and hit an abandoned house. There is so much more to the state than red clay soil and cotton fields. In this particular region of the state, the cotton fields were a nice common theme for my work that day.

After driving down several different backroads and developing my sense of true north in the area, I found myself approaching civilization, as in a few businesses and intersections with stoplights. I either needed to keep going or turn around and try different roads. During my time of indecision, I saw a burnt down brick house, and almost missed this little abandoned storefront next to it, buried in the overgrown vegetation.

This building was small and charming, very reminiscent of an old-time gas station or general store. Later, I was able to find some answers.

The wide inside view of the building tells an interesting story. Random belongings were left behind without much of a system to the type of contents. The residential style kitchen tells me the old store probably had a breakfast and/or lunch counter and sold sandwiches.

Right: If this doesn't scream "old gas station bathroom" I don't know what else would. I would be lying if I said I've never used one of those abandoned building toilets—the water has to go somewhere.

Below: I love old electrical boxes, especially with hanging wires and surface rust/patina on them.

The mystique and anonymity of this little building made for an interesting but quick stop. The burnt down brick building next to it caught my attention first. I was able to do a little bit of local intel after I visited the area. The small storefront was a roadside general/grocery store that backed up to railroad tracks that are no longer there. Often the railroad in those days was used to restock all kinds of establishments. The old store has been abandoned since the 1950s, maybe 1960s. I thought the brick building was a church, but I'm told it was a house.

This steak was cooked well done, actually charred!

3

FARMHOUSE FOLKLORE

In the final moments of my exploration before returning home, I found access to a service road that ran parallel to the interstate, and was approaching a dead end in the road. Lo and behold, I saw a very old abandoned farm house sitting in the middle of a field, surrounded by vegetation. I knew I had to go explore. I walked through the freshly bush hogged cotton field at the end of its harvest to approach the house. The stalks of cotton plants sticking up from the ground required careful footing. It was all open, flat land, with a far away horizon line. Because nothing obstructed the view, I wanted to work as quickly as possible on the outside of the house. The house may have been abandoned for a long time, but the land was active.

At one time, this home was a welcoming sight for family and visitors. In its present state, it was a welcome sight for me, as this was exactly what I was looking for.

That front porch area facing this side was my only point of entry. It was as shaky as you can imagine by looking at this picture.

As I made my way around the perimeter of the house, I saw some abandoned farm equipment sitting in the weeds. There was a neighboring house on the other side of the tree row, and their dog barked when they heard my footsteps through the brush. I knew I needed to focus on the inside if I could get in without falling through the floor.

The other side of the house, with no clear entrance because of trees that took their rightful place back from the house that was their oppressor.

I walked across the floor joists on the front of the house to get inside. It felt like walking on rotted logs in the forest. I think it was worth the risk, even though I was alone.

The covered front porch seemed to serve as a utility room, too.

Above: The kitchen was amazing! I guess I was about 3 decades too late for granny's famous chicken and biscuits.

Right: I explored an abandoned farmhouse and learned a wise tale I'd never heard before. I think, because it was placed over the kitchen sink, it was a passive aggressive way to say, "Don't let the dishes pile up, wash as you go and avoid a mess." Clever.

Above left: The tree telling the house it was there first.

Above right: The inside view of the front porch, which was my access point. I realized that getting out was harder than getting in. At that point, I could hear my friend Jerry telling me I shouldn't have gone in. No risk, no reward.

Outdated furniture in the living room, which was not easy to get to.

Right: I could have pole vaulted to the other side of the house I suppose.

Below: A rusted saw blade sitting on top of a 1987-88 phone book! This gives us a clue for the timeline of the house's abandonment.

Above left: I stood in the covered porch area and was very still. None of my exit options were particularly good.

Above right: It was a tense moment, but I got out, and was admiring some fallen roofing materials.

I suppose even irrigation system wheels have their useful life.

Once I exited the old falling farm house, I looked across the vast cotton field and saw a few men on an adjoining farm property. If they were closer, I'd probably have talked with them, but it was a comfortable distance to quietly exit and an uncomfortable distance to approach. I walked along the tree row on the far side of the property and saw a bunch of old wheels from an irrigation system sitting in the weeds. This was a high note to end the journey on and drive off into the sunset.

4

THE ASYLUM

After having lunch with my niece in Birmingham, my friend Jerry Winnett and I went on a mission to find the abandoned Old Bryce insane asylum in Northport, outside of Tuscaloosa. We knew the structure would not be easy to find, and was abandoned for a long time, but had no idea just how deep and disturbing some of its history really is. We also did not know the true identity of the building we were headed to. With some persistence, we turned down a very long straight and narrow crater-filled private road surrounded by tall weeds. At the end of this dark, creepy road sat perhaps the most demonic structure we have ever set foot in.

We navigated (very carefully) through the badly deteriorated three-story institution, and down its dark hallways and stairways, only to wallow deeper and deeper into a new level of pure destruction. Several inches of dirt covered the floors and stairs from years of vacancy. The roof was badly deteriorated, even missing in spots. Building rubble and other garbage was under our feet through the entire inside journey. Layers of plaster and tile were falling from the walls that were completely covered by bad graffiti and other extensive vandalism over the decades.

Above: The front view of the asylum that awaited us as we arrived. Right then, we knew this was well worth our drive. Thankfully, no police were there to quash our long-awaited excursion.

Right: The pillars and front entrance loaded with peeling paint, climbing vines and growth, and graffiti.

The stairwell that goes to the second level.

The back view of the building from the open window. There was little or no window glass still in place in the entire building.

Above: A look down at the basement level that had inches of standing water.

Right: The unsettling looking stairwell, resembling a school fire escape.

There were many rooms in the building—most looked the same due to the effects of time, reclaiming of nature, and vandalism.

Some fallen ductwork on the back side of the building, first floor.

One of the large open rooms with earth covering the floors. It's a wonder the floors were that strong.

Freedom of expression.

Because this stairwell didn't look one single bit questionable, we took it to the second level.

Moss was growing, no rolling stones here.

The view from the second-floor window, overlooking the first floor roof.

The only tub I found in the whole place. Furnishings and belongings were nonexistent by now. But the level of distress is the best it's ever been.

Left: A guard from the staircase down a long dark hallway on the second floor, where I could feel water dripping on my head through the upper floor.

Below: This was one of the few window-lit areas where we didn't need a flashlight to navigate the treacherous conditions.

Above: The staircase to the third floor, which we didn't take because it was dark. But we eventually found another way.

Right: The devilishly spooky hallway where we could almost hear the screams of the patients, pounding on the walls, and the ghosts of yesteryear pass us by as we documented the skeletal remains.

Above left: An exterior door at the iron exterior staircase. I think you know where we went from there.

Above right: The gateway to the third floor. There was no roof over most of it and the floor was bad enough to see part of the second floor below it. There wasn't much up there except makeshift rooftop and a few skeletal walls. Sometimes you have to be smarter than the building so it doesn't claim you.

Left: A creepy door with many layers of paint.

Above: Finally, some more fitting graffiti, implied blood splatter.

Right: These may have been some original institutional mattresses.

This hallway, and eventual exit from the first floor. It had perhaps the best condition of any room inside the building.

A part of the back of the asylum, with an old service road.

Above: I'd say this was an old utility building to keep farming and maintenance equipment. Located through more brush behind the main building. More of the story coming.

Right: This old flip-out window was the only form of air conditioning.

The interior was strewn with debris and litter.

The texture and patina on the walls, with funky retro paint colors, makes an interesting subject in itself.

This is the only medical equipment present—isn't this eerie?

Above left: More standing water at another basement level entrance.

Above right: One entrance is as inviting as the other.

Left: A fallen steam pipe that went between the boiler building and the institution.

Below: We were approaching the boiler building.

Some boiler tanks seem to be missing—probably internal, because of the sheer size of them.

Above left: No way out, trapped forever!

Above right: The old tank connected the boiler to these turbines that generate the heat to the building.

At first Jerry and I wondered if this was an in-house crematorium. Boilers fueled by oil, coal, or maybe, people!

The far side of the rear of the building, covered in vegetation. Winter helped the visibility at least some.

Right: That haunting road that brought us in.

Below: A wider view of the front entrance. We walked down the other side of the service road and saw other buildings. This was the gift that kept on giving!

Now I'm about to tell you the history of the property that I know, after doing a lot of collective research. The day we were there, we thought this was the main Old Bryce Hospital, a mental institution built in 1861. The original hospital ceased operations in 2009. The hospital expanded with several annexed properties by the 1920s due to an increased number of resident patients. This particular property was the Jemison Center, built in 1939. It was referred to as the "State Farm Colony For Negroes" since the facilities were segregated during the Jim Crow era. Capable patients worked the plantation to grow food for the facility and take care of basic maintenance needs. The day we were there, we had no idea the deep level of oppression that took place, right where we explored and walked.

Little was known about mental illness in earlier days especially, but the facility under the leadership of director Peter Bryce was quite reputable. Patients were encouraged to enjoy gatherings and theater performances, even to write for the newspaper, *The Meteor*, in the late 1800s. The use of shackles and straightjackets were discouraged for the first time. Over the years, conditions grew crowded and satellite locations were built. This created a demand that the system couldn't keep up with. With growing numbers of mentally ill patients, limited staff, limited funding, and many other setbacks, conditions closely resembled concentration camps. Abusive treatment, dirty conditions, food shortages, and other limited resources created huge deficits and problems within the system. These shortfalls not only meant dramatically declining quality of care, but poor record keeping.

In 1977, the Jemison Center closed, because segregation was finally disallowed. On the same property, adjacent to the main building, in the 1950s, the S. D. Allen intermediate care facility was built as another annex of the Bryce mental health system. It remained open until 2003. All rooms were tile. My mind assumes the worst as to why, but I found no supporting evidence. I will take you through yet another haunting exploration through there. Many speak of the abandoned complex being haunted, and I wouldn't doubt it. This was forty-two years of abandonment at the time of this excursion. Between natural takeover, vandalism, arson, years of decay, storm damage, and the disturbing, controversial history, this was one mind-boggling stop—one we will never forget.

A corridor view of the S. D. Allen Intermediate center, with the outside surrounded by brush.

The outdoor courtyard between wings of the building.

Above left: One of the few rooms without tiled walls.

Above right: A hall closet mop bucket, because nothing could be loose and accessible to dangerous mentally ill patients.

This looked like an old school at first. But not much learning happened here.

There was an unsettling feeling to this building as well.

The graffiti was still not fantastic, but it was improving.

I'm not sure whether this roof was removed by man or natural disaster. But it's off!

Visiting hours are over, I'm afraid.

There you are, Satan graffiti artists, I knew you were here somewhere.

The parting outside view.

5

AMERICAN AS APPLE PIE

This Alabama backroad adventure started off on a rather unusual note. Jerry joined me on the journey, and our first stop was a large and very old abandoned house in the Danville area, sitting back in the weeds. The house was secure, and there was no way in, so we decided to move on. An older neighbor lady next door asked us if we knew the lady who used to live there.

The neighbor told us that she was admitted into a nursing home and believes she was a hoarder. The medic confirmed to her the horrid and dangerous conditions of the house. I think the lady was encouraging us to find a way in because she was curious as well—which is funny, but not a good idea under any circumstances. In those small towns, people talk and they know more than what most care about in larger cities. Nonetheless, it was a pleasant visit and random bit of information.

A bit further down the two-lane backroad in Lawrence County sat a nostalgic general store with antique gas pumps and all kinds of vintage signs. It immediately caught my attention. This was true Americana, a genuine taste of the South and of Alabama. Local intel informed me that the old storefront has been there at least forty years on private land facing the street. Some believe it's a replica, and was never an actual store. If so, this general store is so well done, it was difficult to tell. One tobacco store sign and old gas pumps mixed with the slightly newer design are the only things out of place. There were no trespassing signs leading up to the store, but I couldn't resist.

Above: I couldn't think of a better place to sit on rocking chairs and chew the fat with locals.

Right: In the days of full-service gas stations, customers told the attendant how much gas to pump. Then the attendant hoped it didn't go one cent over, or they would have to cover it.

The RC Cola machine was in beautiful condition, with old pull-out bottles with a built-in bottle opener on the machine.

Some fine classic memorabilia.

I vaguely remember those S&H Green Stamps. Stores give them out based on how much you spent. Then you accumulate stamps until you have enough to buy things you want. It was a way to get shoppers to spend more than usual and pay for that toaster many times over.

Above left: I have seen many more outhouses in Tennessee and Kentucky than in Alabama. Maybe tornadoes have taken more away in Alabama since there are more storm shelters and tornadoes there.

Above right: These are classic manual wash tubs with clothes wringers.

6

POUR YOURSELF A DRINK

I've had my most favorable results in Alabama by getting far away from the interstate and going as deep in backroad exploration as possible. After a combination of backroads, we drove through twenty miles or more of a national forest territory, which was desolate and creepy, even in the daytime. While driving through Winston County, we were starting to find more of what we were looking for. I spotted this old farmhouse in my peripheral vision. With a quick turn up the country road and a walk up the hill, we approached this charming old farmhouse with an oxidized tin roof and native limestone chimneys. I knew we were getting deep enough in rural Alabama to find abandoned treasures with rich character.

It was windy and overcast, but this neglected farmhouse was still an inviting sight.

The long view up the front porch would only reveal an old electric box fan.

The front porch railings were no longer intact. The front door was shut by looping a coat hanger between the doorknob and outside window frame—exactly where it was when we left.

The kitchen table still has literature sitting on it. There were several calendars left behind, dating back to 2004 and 2006.

It was funny seeing my reflection in this TV. I'd have never expected to walk into an abandoned house and see myself on TV.

An interesting shape and size for a gas stovetop.

I'm almost curious if those soda bottles were from past inhabitants or visitors since then. There was no vandalism I could see, so I'm guessing visitors have been few, or maybe we were the first.

Housekeeping is falling down on the job, I see.

1960s or 70s Electrolux canister vacuum cleaner—a retro appliance lover's dream.

Looks like someone was multitasking composting and beer drinking, all while cleaning the sink. That didn't work so well.

Above left: Bead board ceiling in the back porch/breezeway area. I should have known better than to open that old refrigerator. Let's just say the smell wasn't pleasant.

Above right: Fireplaces were sealed off. On top of the mantle sat some creepy artificial flowers in old vases. The few clues left behind pointed to the house being close to how granny left it.

7

LIFE ON THE FARM

From the two-lane Marion County, Alabama, blacktop road we were traveling, I could see remnants of a toppling farmhouse from afar. It was literally surrounded by farmland, complete with cattle and very large hay bales. We navigated down the narrow gravel backroad to investigate this abandoned abode, only to receive the most genuine farmhouse experience to date.

The very old wooden farmhouse was surrounded by active farmland. The back and sides of the former proud Southern home were fenced off from cattle so the cows didn't wander from the land. I saw nothing else within eyeshot down that gravel road, but the home of the landowner was likely further back. This farmhouse was possibly the former home of the landowners' grandparents or other previous generations, still standing for nostalgic and sentimental purposes, despite its advanced state of distress. What the house was lacking in structural soundness it made up for in character and personality.

Floorboards were weak in parts, belongings left behind were few, and parts of the house were ready to crumble, but it still stood. That's a testament to how well built the house was, which was possibly 100 years or older. Given the fact that the house was surrounded by open land, and Alabama is known for tornadoes, that only speaks volumes about its build quality even more. Cows alerted whoever would listen that friendly strangers were lurking. We just gently explored and got the photos we wanted, then continued our excursion.

Now you see why we didn't know at first whether this was a barn or a house. The hay bales threw us off, but the windows gave it away.

This was the best view I could get of the back of the house, leaning against barbed wire fence. Livestock was on the other side, and their presence was seen, heard, and smelled. They have beautiful land and animals.

These front doorsteps showed creativity and ingenuity.

The wide view of the front of the house, in which you can see irregularities.

Those boards with nails up were something to avoid, but we also passed on the slumber party invitation.

Not one, but two chairs that are so ugly, they're interesting.

This may be a very old sleeper sofa.

The light leak reveals the house and chimney separating. But the yellow-green carpet is still intact!

Above left: This may be the oldest television I've run across. An antique enthusiast I know told me it's a 1950s (likely late 1950s) HP.

Above right: The kitchen falling off into the abyss. This is the same side of the house as the chimney with the light leak around it.

Between two fireplaces and this Warm Manning heater, this house stayed warm in the winter. I doubt this house ever saw an air conditioner due to its age and length of abandonment.

This was the view out the front door. It was nice of them to leave a path for our entrance and exit.

Our timing was good to find this remarkable old farmhouse still standing. Maybe the hay bales help protect it from the wind?

8

YESTERDAY'S NEWSPAPER

On the road to Lamar County, Jerry and I spotted a house in the woods, with no sign of a driveway. If this wasn't in the middle of winter and trees were in bloom, we never would have been able to see this old house nestled deep in the woods. Getting to abandoned houses can be problematic as it is, with thorn bushes that never die and dormant brush. In the non-winter months, it's much thicker. There was definitely a story here, and it was time for us to gather clues and put it together. This was a remote area with no nearby neighbors, and you'd be lucky to find nearby gas or stores.

Asphalt siding was a trend in the 1940s and early 1950s, but I think that was an add-on or a remodel from that era. I believe the house was older than that. The floor was in rough shape, and there was debris littered all over the inside of the house, mostly old clothes. Besides a creepy old baby crib and a lot of newspaper, there weren't many belongings left behind. Upon closer look, the newspaper contents I found were from a senior citizens paper from 1973! It was still in perfect condition, and seemed untouched—until it was discovered forty-six years later.

That clue told me that the house was occupied by a senior citizen in the early 1970s, and may have been a shut-in. The crib tells me they probably had grandchildren. Older people, especially in the past, weren't the best at doing wills, life insurance, and making other legal arrangements. It's possible that if this is the case, heirs never did anything with the house and the land, or else it's owned by the state. The newspaper told the best part of this story, and made this a fun visit.

Through the woods, to grandmother's house we go.

Above left: Old clothes, old mail, and old literature. I could have examined mail and done name research from that, but genealogy isn't what I do.

Above right: In this setting, this old crib looked so creepy and institutional.

Someone did a lot of canning.

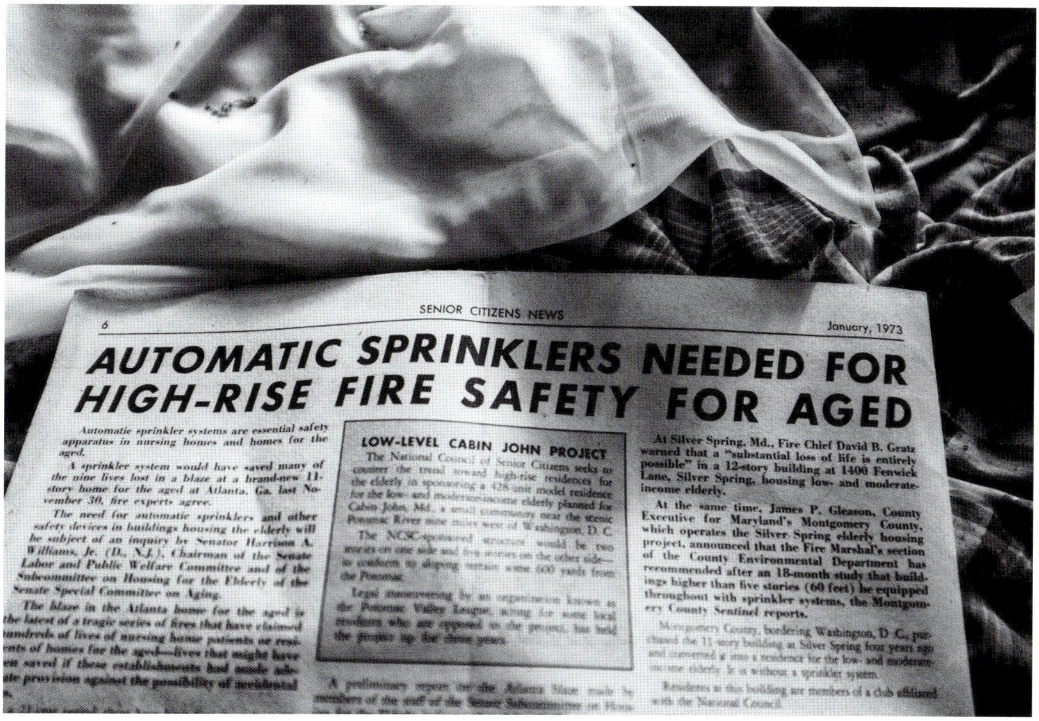

This is one valuable clue I'm glad I paid attention to.

9

THE VICTORIAN INN

Soon after entering into Lamar County, we approached a small town with a gas station, general store, maybe two churches, and a town hall, complete with police and fire. No one was around, which wasn't surprising. Usually when approaching "civilization," the first instinct is to either look for backroads away from it, or go through it and see what lies ahead. We did both, but first, we had to see what the story was with this remarkable Victorian mansion that sat on top of a hill, appearing to be abandoned for ages.

The workmanship and details in the construction of this house were incredible. The inside had 1960s-era (or older) carpet covering the gorgeous wood floors this mansion would undoubtedly have. The contents were few, and the floors were in surprisingly good condition, until reaching the back part of the house. A deteriorating roof was responsible for caved-in floors and a collapsing staircase.

I reached out to the Lamar County Historical Society for information on this grand Victorian mansion. It was built around 1880. That family opened up a mercantile next door. The house was also used as a ten-room inn, where traveling salesmen, known as drummers, would stay. Attached to the property were many acres of farmland to self-sustain the household and help the community. The house employed resident cooks and housekeepers. The kitchen was in the back of the house to avoid heating the living quarters in hot months. Fruits and vegetables were often stored in the basement level to preserve them. Baths were given to the children in the kitchen on Saturday nights. A deep well always provided cold water for guests and townspeople.

The different families who owned the property took great pride in the appearance of the house, its grounds, the gardens, and its reputation in the eyes of townspeople.

Along with a blacksmith shop, the mercantile, tannery, sorghum mill, sawmill, a medicine man, and other community staples, this inn and the families who owned it over the years were seen as pillars of the community. Its current state of disrepair contradicts its rich history.

Very reminiscent of a Southern plantation house. So presidential.

A different angle showcasing the ornate details and woodwork.

It almost seems a shame to carpet over the authentic wood floors.

This 1980s-era t-shirt hot iron press for iron-on transfers was a random find, one I've never seen before in an abandoned house.

These very old propane cylinders also made me wonder if maybe at one time squatters used them for heat. If they were newer, I'd wonder if someone was cooking meth in there.

Now we are getting to the part of the house in the worst condition.

Left: Very old golf clubs rather randomly placed.

Below: It's been decades since biscuits and sweet tea were made in this kitchen.

I suppose these days tidying up for guests isn't a priority. It's okay, we're easy guests and we like it this way.

Now you understand why we didn't explore the upstairs.

Above: The back side of the house, with interesting symmetry and textures.

Right: A back window frame kissed by the sun, bringing out its rich texture and patina.

The site of many gatherings, sipping iced tea or mint juleps, stargazing, all in a different bygone era.

10

THE ROAD TO VERNON

Sometimes, documenting the journey with random findings along the way defines not only the area we travel through, but the adventure itself. These things and places say, "This is America" or "This is Alabama." Even if these places aren't my usual subjects for my abandoned series work, it still represents business in rural and small-town America. Perhaps it should all be a reminder to entrepreneurs to be as smart and business savvy as possible and a reminder to consumers to support local business.

On the backroads that connected different parts of Lamar County, such as Detroit, Sulligent, and Vernon, we found several subjects representing Americana of yesteryear. One of the backroads we explored even took us into Mississippi, then we ended up at the town square in Vernon. Featured in this chapter is a defunct used car lot/car repair shop, a closed-down family BBQ joint, a former welding shop, and an antique Chevrolet slowly decaying in an old storefront parking lot.

The lot is bare these days. I bet that office had walls that could tell some stories.

This old hideaway could have had the best BBQ, but how many prospective customers knew about it?

There were some old buildings on the service roads behind the Vernon town square, this old welding shop being my favorite.

The electric meter was still hooked up, but zeroed out. It was like a ghost town around there.

Above: This was part of a metal bending jig.

Left: This is likely an industrial winch or hoist, according to industrial gurus I asked.

The metal shop with a romantic sun flare—a juxtaposition indeed.

After researching this fine Detroit gem, I discovered this is a 1953 Chevrolet Belair. This year was differentiated by the cross bar over the front grille.

I love the layers of retro colored paint and texture.

Even though this antique Chevy probably hasn't driven in decades, someone would love to buy it and restore it. I have seen many before and after photo collections of different restoration projects. This car may look rough, but someone can save it still. The owner may be the one to do it, who knows? It's not eating hay as it is.

11

NESTLED IN THE PINES

We decided to take a different backroad to Interstate 65 while there was still some daylight left, just in case we found something new. Besides, it's always more interesting to change scenery and explore an unknown road. On our way out of Lamar County and into Fayette County, we nearly missed a very old backwoods house to our left, while laughing at the name of a small BBQ joint on the other side of the road—"The Butt Hutt." I give them props for originality.

Though the old house was unique and full of charm, it was camouflaged by the trees and growth surrounding it. Structurally, it was in very rough condition, and required very careful footing and navigation. It was well built, but primal. It's possible that this house never saw an air conditioner or a television, if it's been abandoned as long as I think.

We said goodbye to this backwoods hideaway and The Butt Hutt, and began a long journey through 100 miles or more of backroads to the highway home. It seemed like forever until we found gas or food. That's how we knew we went deep enough in the Alabama countryside to find some top-notch abandoned treasures.

Humble, but built with pride. If we entered a time warp, and approached this house fifty years ago, would they have invited us to stay for dinner?

Above left: The ruined remains of the fireplace that once kept this cozy home warm and toasty.

Above right: One of the few furnishings that remained.

Above left: Someone had a slumber party with a case of Coors beer, and no one had any idea.

Above right: At one time in its life, this mattress was considered comfortable. Not anymore, I'm afraid.

The skeletal remains of the kitchen cabinets.

More cabinets in better condition. I only wish appliances remained.

Above left: I spoke too soon. The view out the back door, through a very old screen door. It's hard to say whether this or the Victorian mansion was the older house. That Marion County farmhouse wasn't far off either.

Above right: A very old Schwinn bicycle frame, consumed by the elements.

Above left: The mildew and moss growing on the back of the house eventually takes a toll on wooden siding, but the house still stands.

Above right: This Frigidaire electric stove manufactured in 1967 was either dumped here or it was used in this house.

This utility barn further back on the property was photogenic, though empty.

This deep freezer and forgotten bicycle were cleverly hidden by pine needles, and blended into the landscape.

At first, we thought this was a well house, but the way it was built into the land for storm protection points to it being a storm shelter.

Time has started to claim this barn as well.

A shopping cart, here? It seemed random, unless there used to be a store much closer than any we saw.

The wide view from the back angle, nestled in the pines.

It was hard to tell if these were couch cushions or a truck bench seat.

MORE BY JAY FARRELL

ABANDONED ALABAMA
VOLUME 1

ISBN: 978-1-63499114-8

ABANDONED KENTUCKY

ISBN: 978-1-63499-056-1

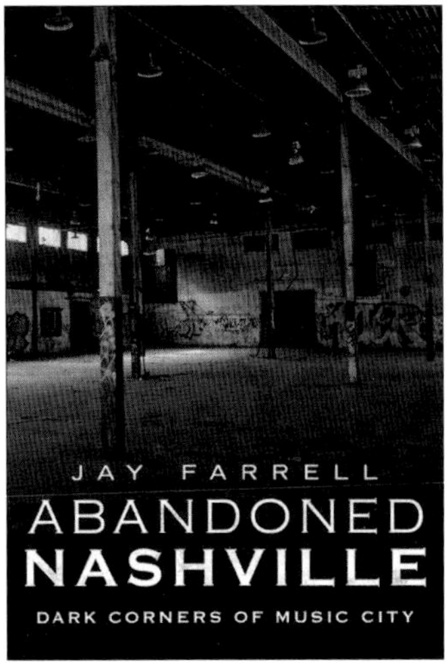

ABANDONED NASHVILLE

ISBN: 978-1-63499-113-1

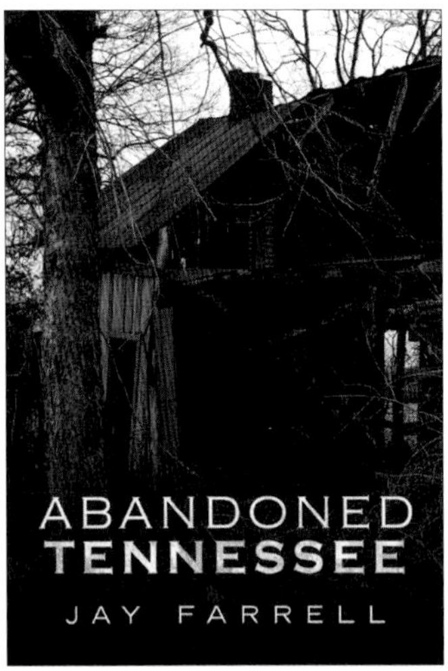

ABANDONED TENNESSEE
VOLUME 1

ISBN: 978-1-63499-055-4

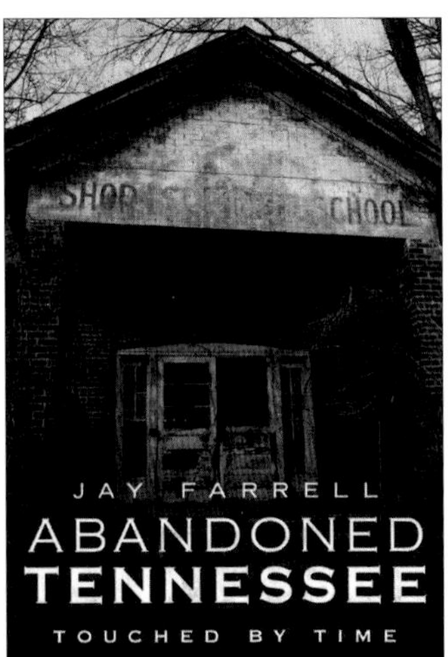

ABANDONED TENNESSEE
VOLUME 2

ISBN: 978-1-63499-102-5